PENNY THOUGHTS

REFLECTIONS ON THE RICHES
OF CATHOLIC TRADITION

BY

PATRICK QUINTON
GONSALVES

Published by

MELROSE
BOOKS

An Imprint of Melrose Press Limited
St Thomas Place, Ely
Cambridgeshire
CB7 4GG, UK
www.melrosebooks.com

FIRST EDITION

Copyright © Patrick Quinton Gonsalves 2008

The Author asserts his moral right to
be identified as the author of this work

Cover designed by Richard Chambers

ISBN 978-1-906050-40-5

Printed and bound in Great Britain by:
Biddles, 24 Rollesby Road, Hardwick Industrial Estate,
King's Lynn. Norfolk PE30 4LS

List of Articles

Introduction

These articles originated from an exchange of e-mails between an older brother and myself. My brother left the Catholic Church and was determined to point out to me that what the Catholic Church teaches is apparently not what is taught in the Scriptures. Ultimately, however, I merely tried to point out to him that he does not have the authority to make such a sweeping statement.

The orientation of most of the articles in this book differs from most books on apologetics, in that the articles focus on the implications of a shift in one's vantage point. The shift is from a private interpretation of a passage of the Scriptures to an interpretation guided by Catholic Tradition. The focus is on the role of Tradition, which directs or guides the process of interpretation.

In general, each one of my replies has focused on one of two issues. Firstly, on the process of interpreting the Scriptures, and the role of Catholic Tradition in that interpretation. Otherwise, on sibling interaction, where an older sibling is insistent that their viewpoint is the correct one, and that the viewpoint of a younger sibling is necessarily mistaken. My guess is that many Catholics have been caught unawares by non-Catholic evangelists, with a comment such as, 'What the Catholic Church teaches is not what is taught in the Bible'. Also, I imagine that such a person is in a similar position to that of a younger sibling caught unawares, by a similar comment from an older sibling. Hence my inclusion of articles on sibling interaction in this collection. In both cases, the dumbfounded listener has the right to question the source of the apparent 'authority' behind that comment.

With regard to the interpretation of the Scriptures, there are two positions: the one is the Scriptures, and the other is the Truth. One is apparently guided by the Holy Spirit from the Scriptures to the Truth. And that passage from the Scriptures to the Truth is the process of interpretation. And that process of interpretation is guided by and constrained by Catholic Tradition.

My older siblings advised me insistently to join an informal Bible study group. One should join such a group, they asserted, in order to discover what the Bible really means. Also, by joining such a group, then one apparently will not be misled by the false doctrine, the false teachings of the Catholic Church on the Bible. My guess is that, what my older siblings did not realize, is that their viewpoint referred to an unspoken, implied authority of an informal Bible study group, that overshadows the apparent authority of the Catholic Church.

Yet, with all their insistence they apparently did not see the implications of a private inspiration when interpreting the Scriptures. During Bible study, one's interpretation of the Scriptures is apparently inspired by the Holy Spirit. Unfortunately, history has proven that, with a private inspiration and a private interpretation, one may not assume that one's interpretation is free of error. The advice that the Catholic

Church offers, is that one should check one's interpretation against the teachings of the Church community. Anyone who promotes the idea of a private interpretation will dislike the idea of checking one's interpretation against the teachings of the Church. My guess is that this dislike will often stem from a dislike of the idea of an authority.

In the light of those contrasting viewpoints on the source of authority, a number of the articles are commentaries on the authority of the Catholic Church.

I have attempted to arrange the articles in such a way that a prominent theme will connect together a number of articles into a cluster.

According to the teachings of the Catholic Church, every faithful member of the Church should make an attempt, either to witness, or to proclaim the Good News. I have considered offering catechism lessons, in order to fulfil that obligation. However, I subsequently realized that writing suits my temperament, more so than does talking. Hence my decision to write these articles. What served as a catalyst for my turning to writing in earnest, was the criticism directed at the teachings of the Catholic Church.

This book has been dedicated to the Immaculate Heart of Mary. At the age of about eighteen months, I was admitted to hospital for the treatment of the potentially debilitating condition of Tuberculosis Meningitis. In spite of that condition, I was able to live a relatively normal life because of Graces received through the Immaculate Heart of Mary. Those Graces were received in reply to Rosary prayers said on my behalf. For those Graces, I offer a prayerful Thank You.

Chapter 1

Stations of the Cross

I am told that every Catholic Church has a sequence of wall paintings called the Stations of the Cross. I am also told that the sixth Station, i.e. Veronica offering Jesus a towel to wipe His face, is not recorded in the Scriptures. For a long time, the fact that the sixth Station was not recorded in the Scriptures puzzled me. Of course, the quick and ready answer to that puzzle is to cite Saint John, where he states that if everything that Jesus did was recorded it would fill numerous volumes (John 21:25). However, there are times when a quick and ready answer is not really satisfying. Eventually, it dawned on me that, in a sense, the Stations of the Cross may be regarded as the first Gospel, because it was composed a good number of years before the four canonical Gospels were written.

It is customary for a poet to compose a poem to commemorate a memorable event. So I should imagine that shortly after the crucifixion, death and resurrection of Jesus, a poet wrote a poem to commemorate the event. And I can only guess that the poet may have given the title of 'Via Dolorosa' to the poem. One should expect the poet to use his imagination to select the fourteen Stations and to choose the sequence of Stations. A fairly standard convention was to compose a poem with fourteen stanzas or verses. Also, literary convention would suggest that the poet included the three Stations in which Jesus fell. Other Stations that one should expect would be: Jesus is condemned, nailing to the cross, dying, and so on. It is quite probable that there were several poets, and each one wrote their own version of 'Via Dolorosa'. Also, one or more of the poems may well have had more than fourteen stanzas. But that does not affect the overall vision. However, the poem that appealed to the hearts and minds of the people at the time would become popular, would be copied and would circulate widely. The copying and circulation of the poems would have taken place in the first number of weeks or months after the crucifixion, death and resurrection of Jesus.

The canonical Gospels, on the other hand, were apparently written a good number of years after the crucifixion, death and resurrection of Jesus. Apparently, these Gospels were written to preserve the Apostles' firsthand witness of the teachings of Jesus.

In modern times, Biblical scholars claim that Mark's Gospel was the first one to be composed. Apparently, Mark used the so-called Q-source material or sayings of Jesus, as the primary written source to compose his Gospel. I can only imagine that a modern publisher may well have chosen a more descriptive title, such as 'The Teachings and Miracles of Jesus', for the collection of Q-source material. According to the Biblical scholars, the authors of the other Gospels used Mark's Gospel, and possibly additional Q-source material, to compose their Gospels.

I guess that one or more versions of the poem 'Via Dolorosa' may well have been incorporated into the Q-source material.

And it is anyone's guess why a popular version of such a poem was not incorporated into any one of the four canonical Gospels. Fortunately, a popular version of the poem was preserved as the Stations of the Cross. Nevertheless, because the poem 'Via Dolorosa', or the Stations of the Cross, was written a good number of years before the canonical Gospels were written, in a sense the Stations may be regarded as the first Gospel.

Chapter 2

Scripture and Tradition

What is the link between the Canon of Scripture and Tradition? This link has puzzled me because of the apparent contempt for Tradition that is held by many Protestant denominations.

In order to understand what is meant by Tradition, we need to remind ourselves that printing was invented in about 1500 CE. Prior to that manuscripts were hand copied by scribes onto parchment and paper scrolls. At first, individual scrolls would be hand copied and circulated more or less freely among the early Christian community. Only much later would the scrolls or manuscripts be bound into a single volume. Under these circumstances, there was no distinction between canonical and non-canonical writings. The two categories were intermingled and circulated freely.

I should imagine that many of the scrolls would have included commentaries on other writings, principles and techniques of interpretation, recognizing the possibility of inspiration, and in general, guidelines for developing an appreciation of the religious writings.

At some point, the Church at the time was challenged to produce a list of canonical writings or the Canon of Scripture. In my mind's eye, I can imagine a bishop sitting down with a large pile of scrolls. He would be required to decide which scrolls should be included in the Canon of Scripture and which ones should be excluded. The bishop would have some idea of which writings were circulated widely, which of them were edifying and which of them were commonly acknowledged as inspired. All of these factors would be considered when deciding whether or not a scroll should be included in the Canon. I guess that at first the bishop had only a vague idea of which scrolls should be included in the Canon. As he worked through the pile of scrolls he would have a more clear idea of which scrolls should be included in the Canon. So in a sense, the bishop did not simply list the Canon, but he would have discovered the Canon of Scripture. Also, this process would have been carried out by more than one bishop in more than one locality. But that does not affect the overall picture of what happened, nor what was eventually included in the Canon.

The bishop would have gone through the pile of scrolls and perhaps placed what he considered the Canon of Scripture on his right and the non-canonical writings on his left. I should imagine that he would have placed the correct manuscripts on his right.

The entire collection of scrolls, both the canonical and the non-canonical collections, would be the Tradition that was committed to writing. Separating the Canon of Scripture from the non-canonical writings does not now remove the Scriptures from Tradition. The Canon of Scripture would still be part of Tradition. Under these circumstances, the Canon of Scripture is the core or kernel of that part of Tradition that was committed to writing. And Tradition is not now some arbitrary authority standing in opposition to the Scriptures. Scripture and Tradition would still be speaking with a single voice.

After some time, after the bishop had sorted the scrolls, and with a sigh of relief, he would say a prayer of thanksgiving. Now I can imagine an onlooker walking up to the bishop, picking up the collection of scrolls on the bishop's right, the discovered Canon of Scripture. I can also imagine the onlooker saying to the bishop, that he, the onlooker, now has the Canon of Scripture and that he does not need all that riff-raff on the bishop's left, the remainder of the so-called Tradition. Nevertheless, I do wonder if the onlooker would develop a sense of appreciation of the Scriptures without the support of that Tradition.

Returning to the initial question of what is the link between the Canon of Scripture and Tradition, to my mind, the Canon of Scripture is the core or kernel of that part of Tradition that was committed to writing. Also, the Canon of Scripture and Tradition will speak with a single voice, because the Canon was nurtured by and is the fruit of Tradition.

Chapter 3

Catechism of the Catholic Church and Tradition

I am told by Protestant commentators that the Catholic Church uses the Catechisms of the Church to indoctrinate, or brainwash the faithful. Yet, I am also told, even by Catholic commentators, that when one considers the art of writing catechisms, then Martin Luther was a master craftsman of that art. Even Martin Luther found it necessary to write catechisms to clarify the teachings of the Scriptures. So, I am rather unwilling to accept the point that Martin Luther wrote catechisms in order to enlighten his faithful, while the Catholic Church went to the trouble of writing catechisms merely to hoodwink their luckless faithful.

Nevertheless, when one considers the situation of the early Church, then one finds that catechesis was directed primarily at adult converts into the faith. Those converts were taught one of the baptismal creeds, somewhat comparable to our Apostles'

Creed. The catechesis of those converts included explanations of each of the clauses of their respective creeds. It appears that, in time, a baptismal creed served as a focal point of most catechisms. Also, the instructions and teachings that were offered to the adult converts into the faith were traditionally acknowledged to be part of Catholic Tradition.

In a comment made elsewhere, I suggested that the Canon of Scripture is the kernel of that part of Tradition that was committed to writing. Also, that the Canon of Scripture was nurtured by and is the fruit of Tradition.

In a somewhat similar fashion, I understand that the Catechism of the Catholic Church was also nurtured by and is the fruit of Tradition. One may wish to overplay the analogy and suggest that the Canon of Scripture is the kernel of the fruit, and that the Catechism is the fleshy part of the fruit, that surrounds the kernel.

Chapter 4

Why Read the Bible?

I am told, especially by Protestant commentators, that Catholics do not read the Bible. I must admit that, on that charge, I do plead guilty. But I do have three reasons for not reading the Scriptures.

Firstly, we are told in Matthew 13:13 that Jesus of Nazareth spoke to the people in parables and that they did not understand him. Well, I must admit that normally when I read one of the parables, I am left somewhat puzzled and I end up absent-mindedly scratching my head.

Secondly, we are told in 2 Peter 3:16, where Saint Peter is apparently referring to the writings of Saint Paul, that the writings of the latter saint are difficult to understand. I guess that that comment speaks for itself.

From the above two observations, it appears that reading the Scriptures is one issue, but the correct interpretation of the Scriptures is another issue altogether.

Also, with regard to the Old Testament, sections of the

Deuteronomistic history demand more concentration than I can normally muster. Fortunately, there are those little gems in the Old Testament that offer light relief from the Deuteronomistic history. Those gems include Ruth, Tobit and Jonah. I must admit that the book of Jonah, with its somewhat comical storyline, is the one book that I have read from cover to cover a number of times. But I guess that I cannot give myself too much credit for that, because in most modern translations of the Scriptures, Jonah covers about two printed pages.

And the last reason for not reading the Scriptures is that even if we exclude commentaries on the Scriptures, there are a good number of books about the Bible that one can read. The books that have caught my fancy include those that cover the historical background to the events in the Bible, and on how the Bible came to be. In other words how the various books of the Bible came to be written and how the books were collected and collated into a single manuscript.

As an afterthought, I also discovered that the Catholic faith has a long and very rich Tradition which can prove to be very distracting. So, perhaps I should put aside the very interesting commentaries on the Scriptures, written by the Doctors of the Church, such as Saint Jerome and Saint Thomas Aquinas. And perhaps I should put aside the writings of the spiritual masters like Saint John of the Cross and Saint Theresa of Avila, and start reading the Scriptures.

Chapter 5

The Bible Makes Sense

Reading the Scriptures is one issue, correctly interpreting the Scriptures is another issue altogether. With regard to interpretation, what safeguards does one have which will restrain oneself from misrepresenting or misinterpreting those teachings? The issue of safeguards is particularly important, because when one interprets the Scriptures, then the constraints and guides that lead one to the Truth appear to lie outside of the Scriptures themselves. Another related issue is how can one resolve conflicting interpretations either of the teachings of, or of a passage from the Scriptures?

To a degree, safeguards will include familiarity with the Scriptures and a knowledge of the Bible as a whole. As one's familiarity with the Scriptures increases and as one's knowledge of the Bible as a whole increases, then that knowledge can serve as a background or backdrop for interpreting any passage from the Scriptures. And with that backdrop, one should be able to formulate a coherent and consistent interpretation of any one passage from the Scriptures.

The ideal backdrop that one may wish to have, is to be in the position of someone who has read every book of the Bible attentively and from cover to cover, three times over. Perhaps a complementary backdrop for interpreting a passage from the Scriptures is to read a systematic summary either of Catholic theology or of Catholic doctrine.

Judging from the number of books that have the title 'The Bible Makes Sense', I can only guess that the process of interpreting the Scriptures is not at all a straightforward process. What makes matters even worse, is that the Bible itself apparently does not contain a built-in manual containing techniques of interpretation. Admittedly, in the writings of Saint Paul, for example, generally acknowledged techniques of interpretation are used, that one may be able to identify. Incidentally, my guess is that that process of interpreting the Scriptures is a part of what the Catholic Church refers to as Tradition.

Commentators that deal with the interpretation of the Scriptures generally emphasize the fact that there are a number of literary styles or genres in the Scriptures. The commentators also claim that when one interprets a passage from the Scriptures one should choose an interpretative approach that is appropriate for the style or genre of that passage. Also, commentators generally do warn against a purely literal interpretation of the Scriptures. So, when interpreting a passage, then a literal approach may be an appropriate technique, and it does have its rightful place in an interpretation, but should be used with discretion.

Some commentators claim that the authors of the Scriptures were inspired by the Holy Spirit. The commentators also claim that when someone correctly interprets the Scriptures, then that person will also have been inspired by the Holy Spirit. I do believe that that is the case. But, I personally am unable to judge whether or not a commentator was inspired by the Holy Spirit. Even false prophets have claimed that they were inspired by the Holy Spirit.

A question that still remains is: how can one resolve conflicting interpretations either of the teachings of the Scriptures or of a passage from the Scriptures? With regard to conflicting interpretations, in a comment made elsewhere, I suggested that a safeguard that most people use is an appeal to an authority. Also, one's acceptance of the authority of a commentator will be based primarily on trust. Furthermore, the source of that authority that one may appeal to, will lie outside of the Scriptures themselves. For myself, my authorities include Saint Thomas Aquinas, Karl Rahner, Pope John Paul II and Pope Benedict XVI. So, should I come across either an interpretation of a passage from the Scriptures, or any contemporary issue that is being debated, then initially I would refer to the writings of my preferred authority figures to discover what their viewpoints are. And I would use their writings to attempt to understand the issue and to define my own viewpoint.

After one has referred to the writings of generally acknowledged authorities, then one may still feel dissatisfied with one's own viewpoint. Then one's final court of appeal is to resort to prayer. Incidentally, Saint Thomas Aquinas reported that he learned more from meditation and prayer than he did from reading the writings of other religious scholars. A prayer that I have often recited is the following: 'When I read the Scriptures, then in spite of the horrors and human cruelties recorded, please help me to discern Your handiwork and Your guidance in the writings'. In the past, with perseverance and patience, I do believe that my prayers have been answered.

Chapter 6

Jonah's Whale

Just go ahead and interpret the Bible for yourself. The Holy Spirit will inspire you and guide your interpretation. What can one say when one is repeatedly given this advice?

Unfortunately, when I try my hand at interpreting a passage from the Scriptures, then I become stuck on a peripheral issue. Strangely enough, on that score, I am not alone. For example, in the book of Jonah, there appears to have been a lot of pre-occupation with the whale. Was it a whale or was it a large fish that swallowed Jonah? Ultimately, that appears to be a peripheral issue. Apparently, the book of Jonah is a story about the boundless mercy of God, and the passage about the whale is a somewhat incidental event. Much to Jonah's indignation, God was willing to forgive a large city of sinful people. May I remind you, Jonah, that I have some feeling for those sinful people of Nineveh. After all, I was an outspoken atheist for the better part of my life.

Unfortunately, my mind repeatedly drifts back to that peripheral passage about the whale. I am told that the name used in the Scriptures for that whale is Leviathan. I am also told that the author of the book of Jonah lived in a culture steeped in mythology. Apparently, a mind steeped in myth perceived the ocean as Leviathan, a large, formless monster. In our technological age, I guess that the only shapeless, formless creature that we know of is the microscopic amoeba. So, I guess that we can liken Leviathan to an amoeba. An outsized amoeba, to be sure. And a fickle one at that.

And to continue with the story of Jonah. According to the story, Jonah was in the belly of Leviathan for three days. Modern translators will have it that Jonah was in the stomach of a whale for three days (Jonah 2:1). And back to the question of how should one interpret that passage? My guess is that if Jonah was living in the twentieth century, then a modern journalist would have reported that Jonah was lost at sea for three days. To a journalist steeped in mythology, Jonah was in the belly of Leviathan for three days.

So much for the peripheral issue of Jonah's whale. I am told that the book of Jonah is a story about the boundless mercy of God. And Catholic Tradition has an endless series of devotions to remind us of that boundless mercy of God. And the one devotion that appeals to me is Saint Faustina's Chaplets of the Divine Mercy. One of the prayers of the Chaplets refers to the ocean of mercy. The prayer reads as follows:

> You expired, Jesus, but the source of life
> gushed forth for souls and the ocean of
> Mercy opened up for the whole world.
>
> O fount of life, unfathomable Divine Mercy,
> envelop the whole world and empty yourself
> upon us.

The echoing 'ow' sound of the phrases 'ocean of mercy', 'fount of life' and 'unfathomable Divine Mercy' remind me of an echo in an immeasurably large dome. Take the dome, and invert it. Then fill it with that formless Leviathan. Then perhaps, will we only begin to comprehend that unfathomable Divine Mercy!

Chapter 7

Noah's Rainbow

Just go ahead and interpret the Bible for yourself. The Holy Spirit will inspire you and guide your interpretation. What can one say when one is repeatedly given this advice?

Unfortunately, when I try my hand at interpreting a passage from the Scriptures, then I become stuck on a peripheral issue. For example, after the flood, God placed the rainbow in the sky as a reminder for Himself (Genesis 9:13). Apparently, that passage in the Scriptures is implying that God needs a little ribbon bow tied to His thumb, to serve as a reminder for Himself? For me, that is simply incomprehensible!

I subsequently thought that I could only make sense of that passage if I reduced it to human terms. I thought of the scenario where a father had said to his daughter that he would place his favourite pipe into a particular pipe rack, to serve as a reminder for himself. Each time that he noticed his favourite pipe in the pipe rack, then he would remind himself that he needed to buy his daughter a birthday present. In my mind's eye, I can imagine the daughter daydreaming, and staring at the pipe. That pipe is a reminder for Dad! The daydreaming would have come to rest on the word 'Dad'.

In a somewhat similar fashion, when any one of Noah's offspring found himself staring at a rainbow, then his daydreaming would have come to rest on the word 'Father'. That rainbow is a reminder for our heavenly Father! Abba, Father!

Chapter 8

Casting out Demons

I am told that the skill to expound the Scriptures is a charism, likewise exegesis is a charism (1 Corinthians 12:10). I am also told that each person is given his or her own charism as a free gift from the Father. As well, a person may be given the free gift of one charism and may not receive the gift of any other charism.

If I understand the point correctly I should imagine that one may not expect every Tom, Dick and Harry to be able to interpret the Scriptures for himself. Yes, every Tom, Dick and Harry is required to read the Scriptures himself, in order to have a growing familiarity of the Scriptures. But as I understand it, it is advisable to have every private interpretation of a passage from the Scriptures verified by a trusted authority with the appropriate charism.

Nevertheless, I have discovered that I definitely do not have the charism to expound the Scriptures. Normally, when I read the Scriptures I will come across several passages which will leave me at a loss, as I try to interpret them. For example, in several passages in the Gospels, the evangelists had witnessed Jesus casting out demons (Matthew 17:18, Luke 8:26). Now when I attempt to understand that expression of casting out demons I am left at a loss for words. Is it merely an idiomatic expression? At the time of Jesus of Nazareth, was that their manner of understanding human sickness? Their accepted rational and reasonable explanation of human sickness? If they had understood that sickness was the real possession of a person by a demon, how would one reconcile that idea with the idea that each one of us has freedom, the freedom to choose between good and evil?

However, I had noticed that the Apostles themselves could not always cast out demons (Matthew 17:21). When He was questioned about that point Jesus replied that demons like the one they were referring to could be cast out only with prayer and fasting. So every Apostle may not have had the charism to cast out demons. And even when given that charism of casting out demons, they would still need to resort to prayer and fasting to cast out some demons.

Perhaps a point to be emphasized is that casting out of demons is not merely a human endeavour. It requires a leap of faith together with that human effort. And prayer is perhaps, the leap of faith *par excellence.*

My guess is, in the case of casting out demons the process of interpreting the Scriptures requires a leap of faith, together with the human effort. And again, prayer is perhaps the most appropriate leap of faith. An implication of this point is that the process of interpreting the Scriptures is not merely an exercise in persuasive reasoning. The reasoning should be guided by a prayerful leap of faith.

With regard to the prayerful reading of the Scriptures, the writings of both the Catholic mystics and the Apostolic

Fathers of the Church have a strong appeal for me. Incidentally, many of the Apostolic Fathers were mystics themselves. Also, both the Catholic mystics and the Apostolic Fathers are still excellent tutors on prayer and under their prayerful guidance I do believe that they can reveal to me, and expound to me, the Truth contained in the Scriptures.

Chapter 9

Scripture and Literature

C. S. Lewis is one of the many literary figures who made a comment to the effect that the Bible is superb literature. And if there is a single word that most literary figures use to characterize literature, it is 'ambiguity'. It appears that ambiguity is a characteristic both of human language and of literature. The ambiguity appears to arise from the multiplicity of meanings that may be associated with any one image or symbol that one may use. And literature typically involves juxtaposing images and symbols to emphasize specific themes.

Literary critics typically analyze a piece of writing by examining the images and symbols used in the writing. In a somewhat similar fashion, commentators examine the images and symbols used to analyze a passage from the Scriptures. And commentators typically make the statement that 'This extract from the Scriptures means that ...'. Now, that last phrase is a deceptive one. Hidden behind that simple word 'means', is a complex process. The process of interpretation involves a complex interaction of skills and background knowledge. The skills may include that of the analysis of literature in general. Background knowledge may include both the social environment and the literature of the time when a passage of the Scriptures was written.

As one's skills and background knowledge increase, one may discover meanings behind an image or a symbol that may not have been noticed before. For example, one may read about the last supper in Luke 22:14. Some commentators state that that scenario is merely a shared meal. Catholic commentators state that that scenario is also a sacrifice. So, the latter commentators state that the Mass is a re-enactment of the sacrifice of the last supper in addition to a shared meal. Furthermore, those commentators state that the Mass is also a sacrament. At this point, one may ask oneself whether what a Catholic commentator states is merely a flight of his imagination, or a genuine insight that will be generally acknowledged and appreciated by his peers?

For the average reader, one may evaluate the comments of a commentator, firstly, by appealing to an authority, secondly, by appealing to one's own experience and, thirdly, by prayer.

In comments made elsewhere, I suggested that, for the average reader, one's acceptance or rejection of the insights of a commentator will rest primarily on an appeal to an authority. I have also stated my viewpoint about the authority of Catholic scholars, together with my experiences both as sharing in the Eucharist and in prayer. In general, I accept on trust the teachings of the Catholic Church that the Mass is a commemoration or memorial of the last supper. In addition to that it is also both a sacrifice and a sacrament.

With regard to my own experience of sharing in the Eucharist, I have commented elsewhere that sometime after receiving the Eucharist in faith I experience a profound sense of peace. With regard to prayer, I do believe that I have received positive spiritual counselling in prayer. And incidentally, Thomas Aquinas has stated that he had learned more from prayer and contemplation than he had from reading the writings of other scholars. In conclusion, my own experiences with sharing in the Eucharist and with prayer confirm the Church's teachings on the last supper and the Mass.

Chapter 10

Scripture and the Literature of Drama

As I have stated, C. S. Lewis is one of the many literary figures who made a comment to the effect that the Bible is superb literature. He may well have also been a commentator who referred to the Bible as a record of the drama of the people of Israel.

At colleges a favourite question that is asked in an English literature examination is as follows: A passage is quoted from a play. The student is required to comment on the relative position of the passage in the play. Also, the student is required to use the passage to explain the themes that the author has dealt with in the play as a whole.

Since the Bible is primarily literature, one should expect that when a commentator writes a commentary on a passage from the Bible, the commentator may well use a similar approach. The point that I am attempting to emphasize by this illustration is that one can expect multiple themes to weave through any single passage from the Scriptures. A further implication of this illustration is that any commentator on the Scriptures can write more than one sensible commentary on a single passage from the Scriptures. Depending on the intention of the commentator, a single theme may be played down in one commentary but emphasized in another.

Dependent on the intentions of the commentator are the passages from elsewhere in the Scriptures which will be quoted to highlight the theme under discussion. To illustrate this further, it may be rather pointless to write a commentary on an isolated single passage from the Scriptures without referring to other passages from elsewhere in the Scriptures.

It appears that should one examine a single passage from the Scriptures then that passage may have multiple themes weaving through it. Other passages dealing with those themes may well be scattered elsewhere in the Scriptures.

The anticlimax of this illustration is to highlight just why I am rather unwilling to debate a single isolated passage from the Scriptures. Incidentally, this illustration also highlights why I prefer to read entries in a dictionary of Biblical theology, rather than a verse-by-verse commentary on the Scriptures.

Chapter 11

Scripture and Theology

Reading the Scriptures is one issue; correctly interpreting the Scriptures is altogether another issue. With regard to interpretation, what safeguards are in place to restrain oneself from misrepresenting or misinterpreting those teachings? The issue of safeguards is particularly important, because as one interprets the Scriptures the constraints and guides that lead one to the Truth appear to lie outside the Scriptures themselves. Other related issues are how to resolve conflicting interpretations either of the teachings of, or a passage from, the Scriptures?

To a degree, safeguards will include familiarity with the Scriptures and a knowledge of the Bible as a whole. As one's familiarity with the Scriptures and knowledge of the Bible as a whole increase, that knowledge can serve as a background or backdrop for interpreting any passage from the Scriptures. And with that backdrop, one should be able to formulate a coherent and consistent interpretation of any one passage from the Scriptures.

The ideal backdrop one may aspire to is being in the position of someone who has read every book of the Bible attentively from cover to cover three times over. A complementary backdrop for interpreting a passage from the Scriptures is to read a systematic summary of either Catholic theology or Catholic teaching.

The most obvious example of such a summary is the Catechism of the Catholic Church. In a sense, the Catechism may be viewed as examination revision notes for a course in Theology. If that is the case, then one may choose to read any other summary either of Catholic theology or of Catholic doctrine. However, in attempting to choose which book one could read, one ends up at the original question which is when reading about theology, what safeguards are in place to restrain oneself from accepting false teachings or false doctrine?

Fortunately for us, the Apostolic Church Fathers, the early Church Fathers and other Doctors of the Church committed their reflections, both on the Scriptures and on systematic theology, to writing. Those writings constitute a pool of knowledge, which one may draw on for guidance and to clarify one's own understanding. That pool of knowledge will include amongst other writings reflections on the Bible as a whole, generally acknowledged techniques of Scriptural interpretation and systematic summaries of Catholic teachings. My guess is that this pool of accumulated knowledge will form a part of what the Church refers to as Tradition.

With regard to conflicting interpretation of the Scriptures and in a comment made elsewhere, I suggested that a safeguard used by most people is an appeal to an authority. Concerning accepting false teachings or false doctrine when reading about theology, one's safeguards will again be an appeal to an authority. Firstly, one's acceptance of the authority either of a scholar or a theologian will be based primarily on trust. Secondly, the source of that authority will lie outside the Scriptures themselves.

Also, my appeal to authority, in a sense, will be an appeal to Church Tradition. My personal authorities include Saint Thomas Aquinas, Karl Rahner, Pope John Paul II and Pope Benedict XVI. So, should I come across either an interpretation of a passage from the Scriptures or any contemporary issue that is being debated, initially I would refer to the writings of my preferred authority figures to discover their viewpoint. And I would use their writings to attempt to understand the issue and to define my own viewpoint.

Chapter 12

A Commentary on the Scriptures

Is there any merit at all in reading about systematic theology in order to learn about the religious truths that are contained in the Scriptures? Or, can one learn about those truths only by attending Bible study meetings?

One may use the following train of thought to attempt to answer those questions. However, I do think that this train of thought hangs on the question of whether or not a thematic commentary on the Scriptures is a form of theology.

1. Some passages of the Scriptures may not be easy to understand.

2. The truths contained in the Scriptures are not always self-evident.

3. The Scriptures themselves contain some passages which apparently contradict passages elsewhere in the Scriptures.

4. Apparently then, some passages in the Scriptures
   may need some clarification.

In order to clarify passages in the Scriptures, a popular approach used at Bible study meetings is to read a verse-by-verse commentary on the Scriptures.

So, should there be any merit in reading a verse-by-verse commentary on the Scriptures, then one may pose the following queries:

1. Is a verse-by-verse commentary on the Scriptures
   a form of theology?
2. If not, is a thematic commentary on the Scriptures
   a form of theology?

Incidentally, I should imagine that a word-study of passages from the Scriptures is a type of thematic commentary. Also, I should imagine that a difficult position to uphold would be to claim that a thematic commentary on the Scriptures is not a form of theology.

Nevertheless, I think that this point is the watershed in this train of thought. And the third query in this sequence follows:

3. As an alternative to reading a thematic commentary on the Scriptures, is there any merit at all
   in reading about systematic theology to obtain
   clarification on some of the passages in the
   Scriptures?

My suggested answers to these questions are stated in the concluding section below.

Now, to return to the queries posed earlier.

1. Should it be the case that the truths contained in
   the Scriptures are not always self evident, and
2. Should some passages in the Scriptures need
   some clarification, and

3. Should one acknowledge that a thematic commentary on the Scriptures is a form of theology, then ...

   (a) The insistence that one cannot clarify those ambiguities in the Scriptures by reading about systematic theology may be untenable.

   (b) The insistence that one can clarify those ambiguities only by attending Bible study meetings may also be untenable.

So, the conclusions I have arrived at are:

1. A thematic commentary on the Scriptures is a form of theology.

2. By reading about systematic theology, it is possible that one may verify that one's personal interpretation of the Scriptures is coherent and consistent with traditional Catholic teaching.

Finally, the punchline.

Should one acknowledge that a thematic commentary on the Scriptures is a form of theology, then a difficult position to uphold would be to claim that 'What the Catholic Church teaches is not what is taught in the Scriptures'.

Chapter 13

Caught Unawares

One is often caught unawares by comments such as 'The Catholic Church does not teach what is taught in the Bible', and 'No Catholic will be saved, since to be saved, one will need to be baptized and be reborn again'.

Fortunately, for myself, I have learned to be indifferent towards those comments. When I am caught unawares, then I will attempt to remind myself to adopt my first line of defence. That first line of defence consists of five pointers or reminders. They are:

1. I am no public debater, nor a Bible scholar, nor a theologian. Therefore, I need to step back and to have time to think about the details.

2. The interpretation of the Scriptures is a complex, non-trivial process. For example, there are four commonly used approaches to interpreting the book of Revelations. They are the preterist, the idealist, the historicist and the futurist approaches.

Apparently, each approach has its merits, and any one approach does not necessarily exclude any other approach. In view of that, the Truth contained in any one passage from the Scriptures may not always be self-evident.

3. I am unwilling to debate the interpretation of a single isolated passage from the Scriptures. This is the case particularly when one looks at a Bible concordance, when it is obvious that the Bible's reference to any one topic is scattered.

4. I need to clarify or verify any statement about the Truth. My chosen authorities for doing that are firstly, the Catechism of the Catholic Church.

Secondly, Catholic theologians such as Thomas Aquinas and Karl Rahner.

Thirdly, the writings of the Apostolic Fathers of the Church.

5. To discover religious Truths, the approach that I have adopted is to read the Catechism of the Catholic Church, and to complement that with a growing familiarity with the Scriptures.

Also, at the back of my mind, I usually have the question of 'On whose authority is that statement of yours based?' I am most unwilling to accept the comment that the authority is based on the Bible. This unwillingness is linked to the fact that, in general, a single passage from the Scriptures may need to be interpreted, which will refer one back to points 2 and 3 of my first line of defence.

Fortunately, for me, this approach appears to work. However, it does have its drawbacks. If one is inclined to play at public score carding, then my approach will lack popular appeal. However, I am not interested primarily in public score carding, but primarily in discovering the Truth.

Chapter 14

An Appeal to Authority

I should imagine that if I was living at the time when Martin Luther was alive, then I would be in a dilemma. If I had heard one of Martin Luther's speeches or sermons on 'Justification', for example, then I should imagine that his exposition would have made sense and seemed plausible. At that time, Cardinal Kajetan and the theologian John Eck stated the standpoint or teachings of the Catholic Church. No doubt, I would have thought that the Catholic teaching also was plausible and made sense. And even though I was no theologian, I would have still needed to decide which position was the Truth. Both positions would have made sense, but which position was the Truth? Because I am no theologian, it would be very difficult for me to weigh up and evaluate the two positions. I would have been forced to appeal to an authority to help me to decide. Also, the acceptance of an authority would have been based primarily on trust.

Although Martin Luther was an authority (compared to myself) on Scriptural and religious issues, I would still have asked myself if Martin Luther's position was respected by his peers. So, there would be one group of religious leaders, with Martin Luther as their spokesman and another group with Cardinal Kajetan and John Eck as their spokesmen. And again, even though I was no theologian, I would have still needed to decide which position was the Truth. Again, under the circumstances, I would have been forced to appeal to an authority to help me to decide which group was speaking the Truth. I would have assumed that because Cardinal Kajetan and John Eck were long-standing authorities, the position that they were upholding was the Truth. And again, the acceptance of their authority would have been based primarily on trust.

At present, I am neither Martin Luther's contemporary, nor a theologian, but I still need to choose an authority whom I can use to be guided into the Truth. And again, this amounts to an appeal to an authority based primarily on trust. My appeal to authority includes Saint Thomas Aquinas, Karl Rahner, Pope John Paul II and Pope Benedict XVI. So, should I come across either an interpretation of a passage from the Scriptures, or any contemporary issue that is being debated, then initially, I would refer to the writings of my preferred authority figures to discover their viewpoint. And I would use their writings to attempt to understand the issue and to define my own viewpoint.

Chapter 15

The Church Fathers, and Authority

As I understand it, your viewpoint is that each person should read the Scriptures themselves, and that the Holy Spirit will guide each person's interpretation of the Scriptures. Or, if you wish, the Holy Spirit will interpret the Scriptures, and the reader will somehow listen to the Holy Spirit. I acknowledge that there is a degree of truth in that viewpoint. However, I do have queries about that viewpoint:

1. Is there a possibility that someone may have an erroneous or mistaken interpretation of a passage from the Scriptures?

2. How can one resolve two conflicting interpretations of a passage from the Scriptures?

3. How does one account for the existence of a heresy, such as Arianism?

After all, the Arians were able to argue adroitly and very convincingly from the Scriptures themselves. If you had asked a protagonist of Arianism if their interpretation was inspired by the Holy Spirit, my guess is that the protagonist would have replied, "Of course, our interpretation was inspired by the Holy Spirit!" Yet, the Church authorities at that time declared Arianism to be a heresy.

The Scriptures contain the Truth. However, the Truth is not always self-evident, hence the need to interpret the Scriptures to arrive at the Truth. This brings us back to the point of private inspiration and private interpretation of the Scriptures, as opposed to the witness of the Church community. Incidentally, this was also a crucial issue in the Arian controversy.

The Arian controversy was not resolved by referring only to the Scriptures. The Arians were able to argue adroitly and very convincingly from the Scriptures itself. The controversy was finally resolved by referring to the writings of the Apostolic Fathers of the Church.

There appear to be three issues: Scripture, interpretation and the Truth. The Scriptures contain the Truth. And while one is interpreting the Scriptures, one will need to be guided by the Holy Spirit, to arrive at the Truth. The Scriptures appear to be the chief witness to the Truth, but that witness will need to be interpreted. It appears that the writings of the Apostolic Fathers of the Church are an accepted manifestation or representation, by humans, of an inspired interpretation of the Scriptures.

The Catholic Canon of Scriptures is also a part of, and is the fruit of, the Tradition of the Church. The writings of the Apostolic Fathers of the Church are also a highly respected part of the Tradition of the Church. The Apostolic Fathers were also acknowledged to speak with authority on the Scriptures. And it was on the authority of the Apostolic Fathers, that the Arian controversy was finally resolved. Also, the Apostolic Fathers of the Church were responsible, either directly or indirectly, for delineating the Catholic Canon of Scriptures. Their judgment was acknowledged when the Church authorities decided which spiritual writings were selected as canonical. They were responsible for selecting, from the corpus of their contemporary spiritual writings, the Catholic Canon of Scriptures, onto which you are rightfully pinning your Faith.

I hope that this flood of words will explain why I am unwilling to rely entirely on my own judgment to interpret the Scriptures. Instead, to discover the Truth contained in the Scriptures, I have turned to the teachings of the Catholic Church, and to long-standing authorities in the Church.

Chapter 16

Pillars of the Church

I once came across an amusing quip, that every member of a church is a pillar of the church. There are one or two concrete pillars that support the roof, the remainder are caterpillars that crawl in and out.

However, how does one distinguish between a concrete pillar and a caterpillar? My guess is that a concrete pillar is someone who is steeped in contemplative prayer, and who is perhaps also a mystic.

I have often referred to the idea of mystics steeped in contemplative prayer. And unfortunately, I regard myself neither as a mystic steeped in contemplative prayer, nor as a concrete pillar of the Church.

I regard people like Saints John of the Cross and Teresa of Avila both as concrete pillars of the Church, and as heavyweight champions of the mysticism league. And I certainly do not rub shoulders with them. The closest that I have ever come to rubbing shoulders with the heavyweight mystics, is when

I found an empty seat for myself at the theatre, in the foyer! Who knows? Perhaps from that vantage point I had a glimpse of the concert through a crack in the doorway? Whatever happened, I now regard contemplative prayer as the symbol on top of the church steeple, towards which I should be heading.

Nevertheless, I am told that, should one have the appropriate disposition, and with God's Grace, one can reach that destination.

Incidentally, some people have asked me with indignation, "Who are the concrete pillars of the Church?" I should imagine that those people thought that I had some notion of some senior authority in the hierarchy of the Church. My reply to that question was, "A concrete pillar is someone who is steeped in contemplative prayer." But, how does one describe such a person? I subsequently found a book entitled *Prayer. Seeking the Heart of God* by Mother Teresa of Calcutta and Brother Roger of Taize. To my mind, Mother Teresa and Brother Roger are two concrete pillars of the Church!

Chapter 17

Witnesses to the Faith

You may recall that I made the comment that, for the better part of my life, I was an atheist. Then I realized that I was mistaken about the apparent non-existence of God. Also, should I have relied on my own intellectual abilities to interpret the Scriptures, then there was a large risk of myself also being mistaken about my own personal interpretation. And that is why I turned to the Church for spiritual guidance, for the Truth. Also, I looked for long-standing authorities in the Church, such as Thomas Aquinas and the Apostolic Fathers of the Church, for guidance.

Moreover, I also did wonder about the prophets. In the Old Testament, the prophets proclaimed the teachings of God. I wondered if there were modern-day prophets, people who had lived in our lifetime, and who were witnesses to the teachings, both of Christ Jesus and of the Catholic Church. Strangely enough, I did find three modern-day witnesses or prophets. They are Vassula Ryden, Saint Faustina Kowalska and Fr Stefano Gobbi.

Vassula Ryden apparently received messages from Christ Jesus Himself. Those messages have been collated and published into diaries called *True Life in God*. Also, excerpts from the diaries may be viewed at the website 'www.tlig.org'.

Sister Faustina, who died in 1938 and who was canonized by Pope John Paul II in April 2000, received messages from Christ Jesus Himself. Those messages have been collated and published as the Saint Faustina diaries. Sister Faustina was 'instructed' by Christ Jesus to promote devotion to the Divine Mercy. Also, excerpts from Sister Faustina's diaries may be viewed at the website 'www.divinemercysunday.com'.

Fr Gobbi apparently received messages from the Immaculate Heart of Mary. Those messages have been collated and published into a diary called *To the Priests, Our Lady's Beloved Sons*. The organization that promotes the Marian messages is called the Marian Movement of Priests. Also, excerpts from the diaries may be viewed at the website 'www.mmp-usa.org'.

You are welcome to think that these three modern-day prophets are merely figments of my imagination, but their websites are open to anybody's scrutiny.

Strangely enough, the writings in the diaries of all three of these modern-day prophets, are consistent with the teachings of the Catholic Church. For example, all three witnesses confirm the Catholic teaching of the real presence of the Body of Christ in the Eucharist. Also, all three witnesses promote the Stations of the Cross as a devotional prayer. Incidentally, my guess is that when one promotes the Stations of the Cross, then one will promote the use of a crucifix, and not merely a wooden cross, in the church.

Somehow with regard to the interpretation of the Scriptures, I am most unwilling to use my own intellectual abilities to contest the combined wisdom of the Apostolic Fathers, those sterling theologians, such as Thomas Aquinas, and the above three modern-day prophets. Yes, believe it or not, I am most unwilling to do just that!

Nevertheless, the best that I can do is to continue to read about Catholic theology, which I will complement with a growing familiarity of the Scriptures.

Chapter 18

A Slice of Life

The family has arranged a get-together. At the gathering, the family members exchange news and interesting events. On this particular occasion, the family members have agreed to bake a seed loaf. Each family member was requested to bring a handful of seeds and nuts to mix into the dough. After everyone had tasted a piece of their slice of cake, their slice of life, each one spoke about a seed or two that they had tasted.

The youngest sibling happened to speak about a seed that he had tasted and no one else in the family wanted to hear about it. What would typically happen, is that the older siblings would merely negate what the youngest sibling had said. One can imagine the eldest sister saying in a high-pitched, almost hysterical tone of voice, "No! There could not have been a seed like that in the cake! After all, there were so many seeds in my slice of cake, that you wouldn't have been able to even count all of them! So, if there was such a seed, then I would have tasted it in my slice of cake!!" And obviously, this message would have been repeated, with different varieties of spice, down the sibling line.

One thing is certain, that even a professor of Mathematical Statistics would not have been able to convince the eldest sister that statistically speaking, she could never have had a seed of every variety in her slice of cake. The eldest sister would merely have replied, "But, there were so many seeds in my slice of cake ...!"

So, the youngest sibling can only shrug his shoulders and say to himself that if the other family members do not want to hear about that seed, then too bad. Fortunately for the youngest sibling, his opinion is usually respected outside of the family.

Chapter 19

Sibling Hierarchy

In the social sciences, commentators frequently refer to the pecking order of siblings in a large family. One can imagine a fictitious family of four brothers, Abel, Basil, Colin and Deon. Abel is the eldest and Deon the youngest. In primary school, the siblings are very conscious of the pecking order and authority. The siblings should outgrow the sense of authority, but old habits do sometimes linger into adulthood. As schoolboys, the protocol is that if Deon has a query, then he will ask Colin. *Grootboet* (older brother) will know! However, the query may filter upwards to Basil and Abel. If Abel does not know the answer, then he will ask Dad. If Dad does not know the answer, then the query will filter to an 'authority' on the subject outside of the family.

However, when the siblings leave school and go into the world, then in time, the siblings will be communicating directly with those authorities on any subject outside of the family. However, in adulthood, if the idea of sibling authority has not fizzled out, then *grootboet* may still expect *kleinboet* (younger brother) to acknowledge his authority. In the meantime, if *kleinboet* had already discovered a relevant authority on a subject, outside of the family, then *kleinboe*t may not even regard *grootboet* as an authority on that subject. Of course, that may be frustrating for *grootboet*, if he is some imaginary self-elected authority.

We are living in a bookish age. So, one need not even speak directly to an authority, one can merely read their books. And fortunately, books are readily available for established authorities like the Apostolic Fathers of the Church, Thomas Aquinas, Karl Rahner and Pope Benedict XVI.

Obviously, it is more satisfying to speak to a person, rather than reading a book. But what is appealing about books, is that they are available anywhere, anytime. Also, one may re-read a book many times over.

Chapter 20

Contrasting Orientations

The mosaics of our life stories are so very different, that our approaches to the Scriptures appear to differ radically. What I am going to attempt to do is to contrast the two approaches. Hopefully, this will clarify some of the differences between our two vantage points.

In a nutshell, and as I understand it, the following points summarize your approach to the Scriptures:

1. One's own personal interpretation of the Scriptures is important.

2. To rely on one's own intellectual abilities to interpret the Scriptures.

3. An active search for the Truth. In particular, having attended Bible study meetings regularly.

4. Knock and you will find. Knock on the covers of the Bible and the Holy Spirit will show you the Truth.

In a nutshell, the following points summarize my approach to the Scriptures:

1. The Church community's interpretation of the Scriptures is important.

2. I may not rely exclusively on my own intellectual abilities to interpret the Scriptures.

3. Passive discovery of the Truth, which included the Truth contained in the Scriptures. And that, after having systematically read through a series of commentaries on the Sunday Lectionary readings.

4. Knock at the doors of the Church to receive the Sacraments.

5. Passive discovery of the effects, firstly, of regular public and private prayer and, secondly, of receiving the Sacraments of the Church regularly.

The issue of one's own intellectual abilities is possibly central to each of our approaches or vantage points. For the better part of my life I was an atheist. Then I realized that I was mistaken about the apparent non-existence of God. Should I have relied exclusively on my own intellectual abilities to interpret the Scriptures, there was a large risk of also being mistaken about my own personal interpretation. That is why I turned to the Church for spiritual guidance for the Truth. Also, I looked for long-standing authorities in the Church, such as Thomas Aquinas and the Apostolic Fathers of the Church, for guidance.

I slowly discovered that the Church's teachings emphasized, firstly, participation in public and private prayers and, secondly, receiving the Sacrament of the Eucharist regularly. The effects of following those teachings on my personal life are indescribable. One needs to discover, to experience the sense of inner peace, in order to appreciate those effects.

Hopefully, the foregoing will also explain why I made a point of reading the Catechism of the Catholic Church to discover religious Truths. Also, I did realize that I needed to complement the Catechism with a growing familiarity of the Scriptures.

Chapter 21

Analogies and Scenarios

In the articles that I have sent to you I have tried to contrast two approaches to interpreting the Scriptures by referring to changes in one's vantage points. One approach is that of persuasive reasoning and the other approach is that of revealed Truths. And the contrasting vantage points are illustrated by means of analogies and scenarios. Also, in these analogies and scenarios, I have attempted to illustrate the point that, should one habitually use one approach to interpret the Scriptures one may become blind to any other approach to interpret them.

The Church Steeple

Imagine the situation where large buildings are built around an old church with a steeple. And, as is the case with most church steeples, there is a weathercock on top of it. One may be able to catch a glimpse of the steeple through gaps between the buildings. And depending on which building one is standing in, one may be able to see, for example, either the sun, the moon or a star on the weathercock.

Also, living in the area are three rather opinionated sisters, Alice, Betty and Dot. From their respective apartments, Alice can see only the sun, Betty can see only the moon and Dot can see only the star. Because each of the sisters is rather opinionated, each believes that their respective view is the correct one, and that their sisters' are mistaken. One can imagine Alice saying, "Just look out of the window, and you will see that it is a sun on the weathercock." The other sisters will make similar comments about the moon and the star on the weathercock.

Film-makers are very adept at using scenarios to illustrate a point. Imagine the three sisters having a ride in a helicopter. The pilot steers the helicopter to fly over the old church. One can imagine the expression of astonishment on the three faces, when they see that the weathercock in fact has all three symbols of the sun, the moon and a star. But what will leave the three sisters gasping in astonishment, is that they will see that there is also a fourth symbol, a planet. From the helicopter, one can even see Saturn's ring!

The Bible Study Group

Dot regularly attends a Bible study group meeting. Basil, her husband, does not attend the meeting as he is not particularly interested in joining such a group. However, Basil picks up Dot at the meeting to take her home. At the church hall Basil often has a chat with the members of the group, before he and Dot go home.

After a while, the other members of the group notice that even though Basil has never joined a Bible study group, he appears to be reasonably familiar with the Scriptures. When questioned about his knowledge of the Scriptures, Basil explained to some of the members of the group that he had read one or two commentaries on the Scriptures and that he often reads entries in a dictionary of Biblical theology. In any case, Basil usually comments that in his opinion, it is more important to attempt to live the teachings of the Scriptures rather than to have an extensive knowledge of the Scriptures. Basil is obviously happy with his approach and the members of the group respect his choice.

Comments on the Scenarios

1. The attitude of a listener. In a Bible study group, the attitude of a listener is typically passive. The viewpoint of the speaker is respected and the listener attends with interest. Who knows? The speaker may well have discovered a viewpoint no one else in the group has come across. Afterwards one may reflect on what the speaker has said, and may even disagree with his opinion.

2. An alternative attitude. A possible alternative attitude of a listener is to assume a position of authority and to be somewhat critical. The listener assumes that the speaker needs to be corrected and is in need of guidance. In this scenario, the listener may unwittingly not even acknowledge that the speaker has a legitimate viewpoint. Should the speaker have discovered a viewpoint that the listener has not yet come across, then the listener will merely assume that the speaker is mistaken, that the speaker needs to be corrected, and is in need of guidance.

3. The situation of an instructor. In this scenario a
student is speaking to an instructor or a lecturer.
Obviously, the instructor is more knowledgeable
than the student on the subject under discussion.
Yet, the instructor listens attentively, because the
student may well have come across a viewpoint
that the instructor has not yet come across.
Surprisingly enough, I have read a number of
comments by instructors, in which the instructor
has stated that he or she has learned something
from the questions of a student.

4. That steeple. I am going to stretch the analogy
somewhat in this scenario. But I don't know how
else to illustrate the point. The steeple represents
the New Jerusalem. Dot is using the star as
a pointer, as a guide to the steeple. From her
vantage point, the star is obviously the correct
pointer to follow. An element of Dot's vision is
that, unless one joins a Bible study group, then
one may not find one's way to the steeple. Also,
from her vantage point Dot cannot see the other
symbols, so she merely assumes that they do
not exist.

From Betty's vantage point, the moon is obviously the
correct symbol to follow. Under these circumstances, one may
expect that Dot will assume that Betty is mistaken and is need
of guidance.

5. The final punchline. The final punchline is rather
disappointing. In these scenarios, Dot is older
than Betty. Also, my sympathy lies with Betty.

So, in the case of the steeple, Dot assumes that Betty is
mistaken and is in need of guidance.

In the case of the speaker and the listener, Betty is the speaker and Dot is the listener. Dot automatically assumes the position of a somewhat critical authority. And again, Dot assumes that Betty is mistaken and is in need of guidance. Perhaps Dot has never come across the scenario of an instructor learning something new from the questions of a student.

Furthermore, it is possible for Dot to assume the position of an authority, without adopting an authoritarian style. What sometimes happens is that an older sibling, like Dot, will adopt a maternal style, the style of an adult caregiver, when speaking to the younger sibling.

In the Bible study group, Betty's position is somewhat comparable to that of Basil. The only difference is that Dot assumes that Betty is mistaken and is in need of guidance.

Perhaps a point that needs to be explicitly highlighted in this scenario is that people outside of the family respect Betty's (or Basil's) viewpoint. However, an older sibling often does not respect the viewpoint of a younger sibling. Apparently, this attitude is commonplace in large families. An older sibling may not even realize that their attitude towards their younger sibling is different from that of people outside of the family.

It is rather unfortunate that few people have the ability to adopt the vantage point of a fly on the wall, and then use that vantage point to watch their own behaviour.

Chapter 22

Vantage Points

There have been two recurring themes in the articles that I have sent to you. They are, firstly, a shift in one's vantage point and, secondly, a dialogue between *kleinboet* and *grootboet*.

Unfortunately, on both counts, we both agree that we are not on the same wavelength. So, I should imagine that our 'debate' (1) has reached the point where it should be referred to an arbitrator.

For the benefit of any such arbitrator, I would like to summarize my perspectives of the two recurring themes.

The Deceptive Picture

There is an old quip that 'seeing is recognizing'. That picture I sent to you, of an old and a young woman, illustrates the point very well. Initially, one may see, say, only the old woman. One may say to oneself that there is no young woman in the picture.

Should someone manage to point out the young woman in the picture, then every time one looks at the picture one will see both the old and the young woman. Seeing is recognizing. Once one recognizes the two images, one will always see them.

This is the point that I was attempting to illustrate, when I referred to a change in one's vantage point or perspective.

Ultimately, however, one will only attempt to change one's vantage point if one acknowledges that the next person may have a viewpoint or an opinion that is worth considering.

The Deceptive Picture

Vantage Points

Another example that is often used to illustrate a shift in vantage points, is how one perceives the shape of the earth. At some point in history, it was thought that the earth was flat. Subsequently, astronomers and geographers deduced that the earth was round. The shift from the flat-earth theory to the round-earth theory was radical. It was not merely a shift in shades of opinion. Rather, it was a radical change in one's whole outlook, one's whole world view.

With regard to the interpretation of the Scriptures, a shift in one's vantage point is equally radical. One may have the viewpoint that one may use persuasive reasoning to arrive at the truth contained in the Scriptures. Alternatively, one may have the viewpoint that the Truth contained in the Scriptures is revealed to a seer. The viewpoints that one either arrives at the truth by persuasive reasoning, or by Revelation, are radically different. One either adopts the one viewpoint or the other. One cannot repeatedly shift from the one to the other.

A Suggestion from a Subordinate

It is common knowledge that managers are not always open to suggestions from their subordinates. All too often, a company will call on the services of a management consultant, who will interview the employees. Should the consultant mention an employee's suggestion to a manager, only then will the manager consider the suggestion.

A similar concept applies to the siblings in a family. Should a younger sibling make a suggestion then the older siblings will be inclined to ignore that suggestion. However, should a spokesman from outside of the family make the same suggestion, then the older siblings will be more inclined to at least consider the suggestion.

An Arbitrator

In a sense, both the management consultant and the spokesman served as an arbitrator. Both the management and the older siblings were willing to listen to what the arbitrator had to say. I have tried to state my viewpoint, and from my perspective you are apparently not receiving my message clearly and correctly. Again, I should imagine that our debate has reached the point where it should be referred to an arbitrator. In an earlier article, I had suggested that you take my articles to an arbitrator for his comments. Now I feel obliged to repeat that suggestion.

I should imagine that a suitable arbitrator is someone who teaches either English literature or history. Someone who is in the habit of shifting from one vantage point to another, when examining a piece of writing.

Incidentally, you may be interested to know that my own arbitrators are Thomas Aquinas, Karl Rahner, Pope John Paul II and Pope Benedict XVI (previously known as Joseph Cardinal Ratzinger).

I hope that you will be able to find an arbitrator, who will manage to shed some light on my obscure messages. So, for the time being, I am withdrawing from the so-called debate, and I think that I will be in no hurry to send any more articles to you.

Note

1. A dialogue? One or two people have asked me if I have ever considered including a number of my brother's e-mails in this collection. They added that that would create a sense of a dialogue in the collection.

Unfortunately, that idea is not a practical one. The exchange of e-mails was a case of two people talking past each other. My brother never really replied to any one of my questions in my e-mails.

One of the central themes in my e-mails was one of finding an arbitrator to resolve two differing viewpoints. For example, with reference to the real presence of Jesus in the Eucharist, I attempted to explain the Catholic position, while my brother attempted to explain a typical Protestant position. I repeatedly posed the question of who would be a suitable arbitrator to resolve those two differing viewpoints. Unfortunately, my brother never really answered that question.

In a similar vein, and with reference to the process of interpreting the Scriptures, my brother never attempted to explain either the existence of heresies or of the resolution of the differing heretical and traditional viewpoints.

I guess that one cannot simulate a dialogue, when there was no dialogue in the first place.

Chapter 23

Proclaim the Good News

In the later years of my life I became a practising Catholic and was confirmed into the Faith. I attended Mass and received the sacrament of the Eucharist regularly, I received the sacrament of reconciliation all too infrequently and I prayed daily. I tried to pray at least one decade of the rosary and one chaplet of the Divine Mercy daily.

It eventually dawned on me that Catholic teaching is somewhat like a thumbscrew. Initially, when one is confirmed, one is required to make a public confession of faith, of what one believes. This confession of faith is summarized in the Apostles' Creed.

After that, at the next turn of the thumbscrew, one is expected to live according to the teachings of Jesus of Nazareth, as recorded in the Gospels. One is expected to live the spirit of the Beatitudes and under the guidance of the seven virtues. That is a tall order, but one is to try one's best.

Then comes the final turn of the thumbscrew. One is now required to go out and proclaim the Good News. That is a tough one. I am a quiet, shy person and I am supposed to go out and proclaim the Good News!! I had visions of a soap-box, street corner preacher and I thought no! no!! no!!! I don't have the nerve to do that!! So what is one supposed to do? In the end, I realized that I could only resort to writing. Hence my writing of these articles.

Of course, one severe disadvantage of using writing for communication is that there is no immediate feedback. So one does not know if one is getting one's message across to a reader. I simply have to accept that disadvantage and persevere with writing. The situation may be illustrated by means of an analogy of a lamp in the dark. The lamp itself does not know if there is anyone in the surrounding darkness who has noticed it. But the obligation to proclaim the Good News may at least come to rest. Of course, matters may not end there. One may discover that there is yet another turn of the thumbscrew ...!!

Chapter 24

Praying with Mary

One repeatedly hears the criticism that Catholics pray to Mary instead of praying to God. Apparently, those critics appear to suggest that, for a Catholic, when one is saying prayers to Mary, then there is no longer any need for God to be in the picture.

According to the critics, Catholics apparently have not realized that prayer is having a conversation with God. Apparently, one may simply speak to God as one would speak to a friend.

So, prayer is a conversation, a dialogue with God? Fair enough! However, in a conversation, there is a time for talking and a time for listening. The critics of Catholicism tend to focus on the talking, which most people are able to indulge in quite readily. Faithful Catholics, on the other hand, tend to focus on the listening, a skill which most people appear to lack, or it is an activity that most people avoid doing. After all, a faithful Catholic may continue listening, the relationship between God and man is an unequal one, and the human person should listen more than they speak. Or, as an old aphorism would have it, one is given two ears and one mouth, so that one will listen more than one will speak.

My guess is that most people are in a similar position to that of Nicodemus, to whom Jesus said "If I have told you about earthly things and you do not believe, how can you believe if I tell you about heavenly things?" (John 3:12). It is difficult enough to speak to a stranger, let alone to an incomprehensible God. So, my guess is that Catholics will wish to offer their petitions to the person of Mary, together with the request that she pleads on their behalf to Jesus.

Perhaps, a point that should be emphasized is that we Catholics are not praying to Mary, but that we are praying *with* Mary. In a sense, we perceive Mary as running a courier service. We offer our prayers to Mary, who will then deliver our prayers to her son, Jesus. The process of delivering our prayers to Jesus is, in itself, a form of prayer. While Mary is busy delivering our prayers, then we are praying with Mary.

Perhaps, another point that should be emphasized is that Mary was primarily a listener and that she encouraged other people to be listeners. At the Annunciation, when the Angel Gabriel announced to Mary that she would conceive a son and that she must call him Jesus, Mary's simple reply was "I am the handmaid of the Lord" (Luke 1:38). Also, at the wedding feast of Cana, Mary's instructions to the servants were to "do what Jesus tells you to do" (John 2:5).

Perhaps, a third point that should be emphasized is that the focal point of any intercessory prayer or devotional prayer to Mary is that Mary will direct one to the teachings of Jesus. At the wedding feast of Cana, Mary's instructions to the servants were to "do what Jesus tells you to do". In other words, listen to what Jesus is telling one to do, and act on His teachings.

Perhaps, a final point that should be strongly emphasized is that when Mary heard Jesus speak, then 'she pondered those things in her heart' (Luke 2:51). I should imagine that Mary calmed herself, quietened her mind, stilled her mind. After that, Mary listened; she listened attentively to the words of the Indwelling Trinity. Hush! Such is the essence of prayer!

Chapter 25

Living the Bible

Bible study is important. Bible study is very important, it is extremely important. When I make these comments I can see you in my mind's eye, wearing a satisfied smile on your face. However, I have made these comments not merely to taunt you, but because they are unconditionally true.

However, after one has made these comments, there will be a shift in focus. One can then ask, what is the motivation behind the willingness to study the Bible? It is at this point that we appear to part company. One can study the Bible either as an academic exercise in persuasive reasoning, or to establish how to incorporate the teachings of Jesus of Nazareth into one's day-to-day living. So, the focal issue is not about studying the Bible but about living the Bible.

That Bible study is important is unconditionally true. But, what is also unconditionally true is that, should one wish to incorporate the teachings of Jesus of Nazareth into one's day-to-day living, then regular, steady prayer is an unconditional requirement. Jesus Himself set the example. When He was not "busy with my Father's affairs" (Luke 2:49) he was alone in prayer. Bible study and prayer are interwoven.

In comments made elsewhere, I mentioned the prayer that I often recite. It reads as follows, 'When I read the Scriptures, then in spite of the horrors and human cruelties recorded, please help me to discern Your handiwork and Your guidance in the writings'. If I was studying the Scriptures merely as an exercise in persuasive reasoning I may have expected an angel to sit on my shoulder and whisper some profound insight into my ear. Unfortunately, when God addresses us in the Scriptures He assures us that "your ways are not My ways" (Isaiah 55:8).

All too often, God appears to answer one's prayers indirectly. The Truth contained in the Scriptures would be revealed to one of His spokesmen, a seer. One may then be prompted to listen to what a seer has to say. And a seer is typically a man of deep prayer, such as a prophet, a mystic, a bishop, etc. One such a seer, for example, is the mystic Saint Ignatius Loyola who wrote a spiritual guide called *The Spiritual Exercises.* And *The Spiritual Exercises* is regarded by Catholic Tradition as one of the best prayerful studies of the life and teachings of Jesus of Nazareth. Also, *The Spiritual Exercises* is about the application of those teachings into one's day-to-day living.

So, God apparently may reveal the Truth to one of His spokesmen, such as a mystic. However, the revelation typically appears to point to a specific passage in the Scriptures. So the Scriptures, in a sense, serve as a common 'vocabulary' for any revelation. And for anyone who chooses to listen to what a mystic has to say, this common vocabulary will serve as a safeguard to any wild claim in a revelation. The revelation may not contradict the Canon of Scripture. Furthermore, mystics tend to make the statement that they have submitted their revelation to the judgment of the Catholic Church.

Whatever, the only private prompting that I have been vaguely aware of is to pray more and to find out more about styles of prayer. These promptings led me to the writings of the Catholic mystics, such as Saint Teresa of Avila, Saint John of the Cross and Saint Ignatius Loyola.

In comments made elsewhere, I referred to the instructions of the Blessed Virgin Mary, who advised the servants at the wedding feast at Cana to "do what Jesus tells you to do" (John 2:5). So, it should come as no surprise that the Catholic mystical writers also advise one to do what Jesus tells one to do, according to what is recorded in the Gospels.

So, I guess that my prayer about 'discerning Your guidance and Your handiwork' may well have been answered. The answer appears to have been to return to Bible study, but neither as an exercise in persuasive reasoning, nor by resorting to my own private interpretation. Instead, I should return to the study of the Scriptures in prayer, and under the prayerful guidance of the heavyweight champions of the mysticism league.

Chapter 26

Answered Prayers

In the news media, there is often a prayer with the assertion that if that particular prayer is said for three consecutive days, then your prayers will be answered. I am usually left apprehensive when I read that definitive assertion that your prayers will be answered.

I am living a life surrounded by and plagued by human conflict. Because of that conflict, I was drawn more and more into prayer and into sharing in the Eucharist. And yes, I do pray regularly both for the resolution of the conflicts and for peace. Yet the conflicts remain, and hence my apprehension about the assertion that your prayers will be answered.

Nevertheless, during the Mass, we recite Jesus's prayer 'I leave you peace, my peace I give you', and so I yearn both for the resolution of the human conflicts and for peace. However, what I have discovered, is that the more I am drawn into prayer and into sharing in the Eucharist, then more and more I find that I have an inner peace, in spite of the surrounding external conflict. Also, that inner peace has given me the strength to weather the storm.

So, in my situation, I guess that the assertion of 'your prayers will be answered' does apply. But in my mind, the assertion that I repeat to myself is 'your wishes may not be granted but your prayers will be answered in unexpected ways'.

MELROSE BOOKS

If you enjoyed this book you may also like:

The Nazareth Route
Cecil Hargreaves

The Nazareth Route by Cecil Hargreaves focuses on the themes of "challenge" and the "form of vulnerability which consists in a willingness to get hurt and wounded." It is also about human dilemma.

The author outlines as many as thirty people across the world who have been seen to be among Jesus' modern Nazareth 'route-makers' and 'route-finders'.

Size: 234mm x 156mm   Pages: 224
Binding: Hardback with dust jacket   ISBN: 978 1 906050 44 3   £13.99

Across the Divides Chile: A Different Perspective
Gill Williamson Smith

Gill Williamson Smith arrived in Marxist Chile with her Anglican minister husband and their three children. The call of God took them from working among Cockneys in the East End of London to well-heeled, middle-class Chileans and Diplomats, a call tested in the crucible of adversity.

Pre-conceived ideas of those on 'the other side', both in politics and in faith, are re-defined for the author as God is encountered in surprising ways. Tracing the lives of some of those leads the reader to a discovery of far-reaching consequences, both within and beyond Chile today.

Size: 234mm x 156mm   Pages: 496
Binding: Hardback with dust jacket   ISBN: 978 1 906050 49 8   £14.99

Genesis For The Modern Reader
David Bruce Taylor

Genesis for the Modern Reader, by David Bruce Taylor, is an exposition of the whole text of Genesis aimed particularly at a non-specialist readership.

Genesis for the Modern Reader is intelligently, lucidly and attractively written. It will prove interesting not only to the generalist but also to undergraduates and anyone else who wants to know what the authors of Genesis really had in mind. Its scope is wide enough also to offer a useful introduction to biblical studies generally.

Size: 234mm x 156mm   Pages: 448
Binding: Hardback with dust jacket   ISBN: 978 1 905226 47 4   £16.99

St Thomas' Place, Ely, Cambridgeshire CB7 4GG, UK

www.melrosebooks.com   sales@melrosebooks.com